DREAM

BARBIE L. BREATHITT

Edited by Frank A. DeCenso Jr.

DESTINY IMAGE PUBLISHERS

Scripture is the authors' own. Please note that Destiny Image's publishing style capitalizes certain pronouns in Scripture that refer to the Father, Son, and Holy Spirit, and may differ from some publishers' styles. Take note that the name satan and related names are not capitalized. We choose not to acknowledge him, even to the point of violating grammatical rules.

DESTINY IMAGE® PUBLISHERS, INC.

P.O. Box 310, Shippensburg, PA 17257-0310

"Speaking to the Purposes of God for this Generation and for the Generations to Come."

This book and all other Destiny Image, Revival Press, Mercy Place, Fresh Bread, Destiny Image Fiction, and Treasure House books are available at Christian bookstores and distributors worldwide.

For a U.S. bookstore nearest you, call 1-800-722-6774.

For more information on international availability, call 717-532-3040.

Reach us on the Internet at www.destinyimage.com.

Digital Edition ISBN: 978-0-7684-1769-2

Trade Paper ISBN: 978-0-7684-1768-5

Originally published in *Hearing and Understanding the Voice of God*, ISBN 978-0-7684-3803-1.

Dreams and Visions of Destiny

Barbie L. Breathitt

Dreams and Visions of Destiny

Before time began, before natural light existed or the worlds were formed, God had a dream. He spoke across a dark void of emptiness and brought order out of chaos. He brought direction to a vacuous expanse of nothingness. The all-powerful God hung the worlds on the might of His Word. He flung the constellations into space, suspending galaxies upon an invisible structure that continues to expand into the eons of eternity. This same all-knowing, creative, omnipresent God invades the small windows of our hearts each night through the realm of dreams. He takes the formless and void places in our lives and injects His heavenly spectrums of colored light to form images of hope and destiny. He embraces us with words of love that frame our lives and creates endless possibilities for us to explore. (See Genesis 1:3-5.)

Before Adam fell, he understood the mysteries of the universe because he communed with God. Everything God creates is full of His majestic light, power, and beautiful splendor. God's nature is love and He is light. Out of these united substances, God speaks creative words to release life and restoration and revelation into our dreams.

God reminded Job that He was present when Jesus created the universe.

Where is the way to the dwelling of light? And darkness, where is its place, that you may take it to its territory and that you may discern the paths to its home? You know, for you were born then, and the number of your days is great! (Job 38:19-21 NASB)

God etched His promises on man's spirit as the foundations of the world were being formed. God shook Job out of his apathy and depression by restoring revelation, knowledge, and hidden mysteries.

Then the Lord answered Job out of the whirlwind and said, "Who is this that darkens counsel by words without knowledge? Now gird up your loins like a man, and I will ask you, and you instruct Me! ***Where were you when I laid the foundation of the earth? Tell Me, if you have understanding, Who set its measurements? Since you know.*** *Or who stretched the line on it? On what were its bases sunk? Or who laid its cornerstone, when the morning stars sang together and all the sons of God shouted for joy?"* (Job 38:1-7 NASB)

Angels shouted as Jesus, the eternal Word, spoke laying the cornerstone, writing His word upon the hearts of every person. Our dreams cause us to remember who we are in God, the chosen and called. We, like Job, were present in God the day the universe was formed.

The building blocks that form a firm foundation for spiritual growth reflect Jesus, the cornerstone. He gives us the insight we need to recognize our divine connecters. He is our source of confidence. He empowers us to participate in His divine nature and godliness. His power gives us everything we need to have a prosperous life including faith, goodness, knowledge, self-control, perseverance, brotherly kindness, and love. These character traits are all necessary for our spiritual growth. God-given dreams continually work on bringing clarity to immature areas in our lives.

Dreams have a transforming ability if we will respond to their messages and directives.

God's creative promises caused something wonderful to come out of nothing. The heavenly light of God's Word brings insight and creative, color-saturated images into the dreamer's spirit. When God breathes into our dreams, it sets His creative transforming force into action. God's breath gives the spirit of humankind knowledge, understanding, and life. It is by God's grace that we obtain revelation knowledge of the invaluable promises God grants us. These magnificent promises enable us to become partakers of His divine nature.

God's grace and peace help bring understanding of the surpassing knowledge of the mystery of Christ in us, the hope of glory.

Seeing that His divine power has granted to us everything pertaining to life and godliness, through the true knowledge of Him who called us by His own glory and excellence. For by these He has granted to us His precious and magnificent promises, so that by them you may become partakers of the divine nature (2 Peter 1:3-4 NASB).

Dreams empower us to see God's promises manifest. We can then believe what was previously only a fleeting thought. Dreams bring our imagination into the tangible realm of faith. We begin to believe what we see with the eyes of our spirit and with our natural eyes. In this sense, seeing is believing God Himself, who communicates through His Spirit to us through dreams.

God-given dreams carry a creative ability because they are prophetic in nature. God-given dreams come to change us into His image. God-given dreams enable us to walk in the Spirit with a renewed understanding of His vision, purpose, or plans for us. Dreams position us to embrace the promises of God. Dreams are just one of the many vehicles God has chosen to show and tell us who we are called to be in Christ. His desire is for us to reach our full potential and to be successful (see Ps. 24:1).

God-given dreams reveal keys to unlock the richness of life. The closer we come to the Lord, the more we see our need to resonate with the sounds of Heaven, to establish His Kingdom on earth. God has tuned each person like a unique instrument that releases a specific sound or new song in the orchestra of life. When we learn to walk as sons of God, in the fullness of unity (or harmony) with the sounds of the Kingdom of Heaven, earth will respond. God commands blessings upon us as we harmonize with the dreams He designs for our lives.

God has called us as mediators on the earth. We bring Heaven to earth through our dreams, decrees, prayers, prophecies, declarations, praise, and worship. God wants us to cry out to Him for wisdom and understanding. Just as He created the stars to light the heavens (see Ps. 147:4-5), God releases light and sound through dreams to cause His voice to resonate throughout creation.

Our dreams are a gateway for God to visit us. Through our dreams, God separates and dispels the darkness of sin and replaces it with the colors of His glorious light. He eliminates the chaos in our lives and brings us into perfect order to unlock our destiny by painting a brilliant new life story (see Prov. 3:5-6).

Mirror Image of the Creator

Dreams reflect the mirror image of the Creator as our minds are renewed by receiving and applying His Word. If our spirit is immersed in the living, transforming Word of God and is prayerfully developed in its fullness by consistent times of intimate communication with God, our spirit can receive grace to partake of His precious and magnificent promises obtainable through His divine power.

God communicates to the soul of man through dreams. As we meditate on God upon our beds, our souls begin to dialogue with God and He responds to us through dreams that dramatize our intimate conversation.

A dream aligns us with the present moment and reflects our true selves. If we will contemplate our dreams, we will see qualities of ourselves represented by characters or symbols in the dream. Because we are destined to reflect God's image as we come to know Him better, the closer we draw to God, the better we can reflect His love. His light reveals our condition as well as His unconditional love that changes us because we see ourselves clearly. We are Children of Light because our Creator is the Father of Lights. We are called to live a life where nothing is hidden from His sight, and everything is exposed to His light. Anything concealed in darkness will only distract us from our destiny and will eventually cause us to stumble and fall. Dreams bring God's brilliant enlightenment and love to our lives by dispelling darkness.

Dreams enable us to look past the present circumstances of our lives to see the endless possibilities that await our discovery in the eternal realm of the Spirit. The Kingdom of God is invisible because its vastness is without end.

From this eternal realm come visions of the night, which spark faith and release hope for our present, near future, and all eternity.

God projects pictures upon the screens of our hearts. He speaks tenderly with life-giving creative words. If we will embrace these messages with faith and obedience, we will be transformed. If we ignore His dream messages, we will remain the same. Unchanged people forget who they are called to be and risk never reaching their destiny or fully maturing into the character of Christ.

Dreams and Destiny

Dreams are at times a mirror image of the soul. They reflect our inner condition by revealing what will transpire if changes do not take place in us. Dreams are like relationships we maintain with friends. If we nurture them, they will grow and develop. If we ignore or neglect them, they will vaporize and disappear. If we honor our dreams, by writing them down and prayerfully following their instruction, they will become wise counselors to us. But if we ignore our dreams, they will not flourish.

God has programmed every person's spirit with the understanding of who He has made him or her to be. Our spirit knows who we are destined to be and the paths we must take to get there. Our part is to embrace God's plan through faith by cooperating with His changes and trusting Him to take obedient risks in life. To live according to who we really are, we must allow our life's dream to order our steps. God gives crucial directions through dreams, and it's important that we pay attention to them.

Having a greater measure of the Holy Spirit's guiding light also helps direct our lives. God's promises are the foundational laws of His Kingdom. Light-saturated revelation from God causes truth to invade our past, present, and future situations.

Many people are on a quest to discover the reason they exist and their God-given purpose in destiny. God's wisdom is often revealed in the mystery of a dream. The foremost question people ponder is, *What are my dreams trying to tell me about my destiny?* (see 1 Corinthians 2:7-9).

Understanding dreams requires that dreamers develop their spiritual gifts and skills. Our spiritual ears must be tuned to hear the Creator's voice as well as the voice of our own soul as it searches for God. More importantly, our spiritual eyes must also be focused to see into the realms of faith to behold and retain the fleeting images that play upon the screens of our mind's eye.

Trained Through Prayer

How do we develop our ability to understand a spiritual voice when we are so used to hearing the voices in the world dictate who we are and what we should be doing with our lives? There is a renewing of our minds and a changing of our hearts through love that must happen to allow our spirit man to take the lead. The Holy Spirit speaks the Word that gives us life and creates the vision to follow so we can fulfill our dreams and reject the dictates of the world.

How do we train our spiritual eyes to discern the unseen eternal realms that are featured every night in our dreams and visions? How do we sensitize our spirit to know when God has invaded our dreams? One avenue is by receiving His love through prayer.

Desperate prayer caused the Lord to remember Hannah and heal her barren life. The Lord gave her more than a son in Samuel. He gave her a prophet and a seer for a nation. The Lord stood before Samuel in the vision realm focusing Samuel's eyes to see. The God of all creation called Samuel's name audibly several times, tuning his ears to hear. Eli instructed Samuel to lie down and rest to wait for the coming of the Lord. Allow me to paraphrase what Eli said to Samuel, "Acknowledge the presence of the Lord when he comes, and declare you have ears to hear his voice" (author's paraphrase, see 1 Sam. 3:7-10).

The seer, the prophet, and the watchmen of God are coming into a new dream realm of vision and spiritual understanding. God is orchestrating divine encounters. He is pouring out dreams and visions in an increased measure upon all flesh (see Acts 2:17-18).

Visions Speak of the Future

It is necessary to prepare our hearts to see our future and experience destiny in our own God encounters. God reveals the future in dreams so we can prayerfully bring the future into our present. Habakkuk 2:2 tells us to write down the visions God shows us so the message is clear, easy to read, and understandable. Visions speak of a future time that is appointed to come. We will obtain the vision if we believe it, prepare, and continue to patiently wait.

The ministry of the seer brings a major shift from just hearing the Word of God to *seeing* the plans of God unfold in dreams and visions. It is easier to remember a spectacular sight, because it imprints on our soul more than words that echo in our ears. We are visual beings; without a clear vision we remain naked, uncovered, and finally perish.

If we will lie down in peace to position ourselves in a place of covenant rest, God will visit us in our dreams. He may even appear to us nightly in the realms of the Spirit. We are always trying to be "human doings" when God has called us to be "human beings." God wants us to be at rest in His presence to hear His voice, experience His intimate love, and see a vision of who we are in the future (see 1 Sam. 3:11-14).

The Bible is full of God-given revelation through dreams, visions, and prophecy. We study to show ourselves approved so that we can operate in the Spirit of understanding and be spiritually fruitful (see 2 Tim. 2:15). We must learn from the Holy Spirit to discern between good and evil. Godly character will reject the evil and embrace the truth. In Ephesians 1:17-19, Paul prays that believers may be enlightened in our understanding in order to have the riches of God's glorious power manifest in our lives. This means that every believer must be led by the Holy Spirit's wisdom and revelation to understand the Father's heart.

The presence of God residing in our lives enables us to live the impossible dream. We do well to adopt the prayer of Moses in Exodus 33:13-16, when Moses asked God to show him His ways. This involves seeing the spiritual realm of vision. If we are able to see our future and understand the ways God wants us to walk, we will prosper. It is time to see the grace and favor of God resting upon us in the realms of glory. When our love for God and others is overflowing, it will demonstrate the reality of His glorious presence and the truth of the Gospel of the Kingdom.

Wisdom in Dreams

Dreams are like fleeting vapors. They appear for a brief moment in time and then vanish away forever if not captured. Dreams that are captured become a precious treasure from God. We need to ask God for dreams to obtain these elusive treasures and answers. Boldly seek God for revelatory significance that unfolds by receiving His dream messages. Continue to knock in order to acquire the interpretation and then simply believe. The mysteries God seals within our spirits create urgency within to seek after Him for the keys to unlock the treasures He has deposited (see Ps. 9:10).

God loves to use dreams to reawaken us with prophetic insight and to spur us forward toward our destiny in Him. To reach our full potential and God-given destiny, we must always set the Lord before us and stay focused on His plans. We must see ourselves as God sees us and interpret our dreams according to His loving nature, His divine words, and His creative language to us, not according to what humanity says or even what we believe about ourselves.

Dreams are also given to direct us onto the proper paths in life. To discover these paths we must learn to read the sign posts and properly interpret the symbols on our dream maps. Interpreting dreams is more than being able to recall the dream's events. It is being able to discern the wisdom that our dreams contain and apply it accordingly.

Our relationship with God grows under the guidance of the Holy Spirit. As we ask him for discernment, wisdom, and understanding, the Lord will direct and guide our paths, often using dreams to teach us. Without the understanding of our dreams, we can remain in unfruitful darkness, but with understanding we can be saved, healed, and delivered (see Prov. 2:3-12).

God is the only one who knows the future. God has a divine dream plan for us to be successful and achieve our destiny in life. He reveals the paths of success in our dreams, so our hope remains in Him. Jeremiah 29:11 reveals the Father's heart to us. When our lives are diverted from God's planned path, He sends a dream to correct our course and restore hope in a prosperous future. As we pray for understanding and seek His wisdom with a sincere heart, we will find the answers to life's quest. God enables those who remain on His path to be strengthened (see Job 17:9).

Dreams bring us heavenly wisdom. Spiritual perceptions rain down upon open hearts to receive God's saving grace and knowledge (see Isa. 45:8). The dreams God sends speak the truth to us in love so we can grow up into Him. Christ holds the whole Body together and empowers each part to do its work.

In a society where success is expressed through accomplishments, financial stability, and busy schedules, God often talks to us the only way He can—when we are asleep. This may be the only time that we are quiet enough to hear Him. Dreams reveal our emotions, our pain, future events, and even hidden things of darkness. The puzzle pieces that God uses in dreams are part of His divine language. God gives us understanding as He searches the intents of our thoughts and hearts. If we seek God with our whole heart, we will find Him. While we sleep, our soul continually searches to make intimate contact with God. Dreams give us God's perspective to steer us away from harmful events and to give us life, vision, direction, provision, and a clear picture of our destiny.

A scoffer may seek wisdom and find none, but spiritual knowledge comes easily to one who has an understanding heart. Wisdom rests in the hearts of those who, like Solomon, seek to have spiritual understanding of their dreams.

A true dreamer is one who sees the impossible, and knows through God it will become possible. Dreamers are able to see the shadow of things to come as if by moonlight. By joining their faith to believe, the rays of the morning's dawn bring understanding and clarity (see Job 33:15-18).

Our dreams are God's answers to the hidden questions we conceal within. Once the reality of our dreams are embraced, we have the courage and fortitude to give them life and expression. As we bring our cares to God, He delivers us. The Word of the Lord is living and active. It penetrates the barriers of the soul, reaching our inner spirit to reveal the secrets in our hearts. We are laid bare and become transparent; nothing is hidden in its light.

Angels and Realms of Glory

Biblical history testifies that God has spoken to humankind through dreams since the beginning of time. Our dream life is like a highway on which messages are carried to the mind's eye and then to the spirit. These communications may come from a variety of sources: from the business of the day; from the body; from the soul; from the demonic realm; or from God and his angelic messengers.

Angels are heavenly messengers who are comprised of fire, wind, light, and the breath of God's Spirit. They appear in dreams and visions or come in visitations to deliver messages to guide us into God's pure truth.

Angels enter our dreams to bring messages from God's eternal realm. The Holy Spirit hovers over humankind, tenderly embracing us at night while favoring us with dreams that call us to pursue Him wholeheartedly.

God created the principle of becoming what we behold. Jacob grew exceedingly prosperous by seeing and hearing God's plan in a dream and by following the angel's instructions. Divine strategies are created from the dream fibers of moral excellence, character, integrity, and love.

We determine the amount and type of light that we are able to receive in dreams. The white light of God's kingdom draws the angelic realm to us so that we will shine with His light and draw others to His Kingdom. Angels are very active in our dreams—leading, guiding, and helping to direct us to the proper interpretations. The spiritual garments of light we wear are dependent upon the words we speak and the visions we believe. God is able to turn our darkness into His light (see Ps. 18:28).

God's light in our dreams will draw angels toward us. The Holy Spirit trains us to grow in spiritual discernment. He will open our eyes to see the glory realms of His majestic splendor, heavenly creatures, hosts of lights, and the angels. As we speak God's words of life, effectual doors of opportunity open. Words build a spiritual framework around us that form the atmosphere we exist in. We are responsible for creating a positive life by the choices we make and the words we pray and say every day (see Heb. 11:3).

By walking in God's divine nature, we are witnesses to the angelic realms. In John 11:40, *Jesus said to her, "Did I not say to you that if you would believe you would see the glory of God?"* (NKJV). Dreams reveal realms of glory. When we develop our ability to "believe" the things of God with our hearts, and not just our minds, we are able to walk in a spiritual understanding of the mysteries of days to come.

Daniel and Joseph—Dream Ministers

Daniel was known as a man of great godly wisdom with an excellent spirit; knowledgeable, with great understanding, able to interpret dreams, solve riddles, and explain enigmas. Daniel's spiritual intimacy enabled the deep of God to reveal deep and hidden mysteries to the deep in Daniel. No secret troubled Daniel. He was even able to explain the handwriting on the wall (see Dan.

5:24-29). World rulers said of him, "*the Spirit of God is in you...light and understanding and excellent wisdom are found in you*" (Dan. 5:14 NKJV).

Joseph was severely tested by the Word of God until it finally perfected his character, releasing him from the shackles that bound him. Finally, he was propelled into his destiny in front of kings and rulers. (See Genesis 39-49.) Daniel and Joseph were able to accurately discern and reveal mysteries to all who came before them, great and small. Where are the gifted dream interpreters who are called to stand before the Pharaohs of our day?

Daniel saw that the wise will be enlightened to shine like stars, being able to ascend and descend an invisible heavenly ladder as they increase in the knowledge of God's ways (see Dan. 12:3-4). This verse speaks of man's natural knowledge as well as the increased knowledge and understanding of the mysterious ways of God. God-given dreams reveal spiritual truths that have been sealed (see Job 33:15-18). Daniel tapped into God's revelatory realm. He was shown futuristic insights and end-time revelation. Daniel was told to seal up these words until the time when knowledge of God's ways will increase and people will be purged and refined with fire (see Dan. 12:10). Daniel knew how to decree truth and repent of sin to open spiritual gates into the natural realms. Daniel prayed until he experienced breakthrough, empowerment, and revelatory wisdom and knowledge.

Prayer is the Gateway

Prayer is the gateway to the realm of vision and dream revelation. Daniel was visited by the angel Gabriel in the vision realm. Gabriel gave Daniel skill with spiritual understanding. It is important to cooperate with the angelic hosts who enable the spiritual eyes of our hearts to be enlightened to see.

It's no wonder that the process we go through to walk in the ways of God's wisdom are forged by fiery tests and trials that fervently conform us to His glorious image. Those with godly insight will understand dream mysteries and use these tools to win souls.

In God's eternal plan to bring salvation to humankind, He deposited His divine light into each person whom He sent into the world. The given measure of divine light is sufficient to draw every man, woman, boy, and girl back into the "Giver of Light." But each person must choose to walk in the light and allow God's light to bring salvation. Those who refuse to walk in the light continue to dwell in darkness and never reach their full potential or God-given destiny. As true light shines in our hearts we are able to remove the things that cause us to stumble.

Dreams and visions bring about a face-to-face encounter similar to what Moses had with God. Dreams show us the goodness of the Lord's countenance upon us. Through our dreams, He places gladness and peace in our hearts; He shows us how to prosper and live in safety.

God supplied the children of Israel with light in their dwellings while the Egyptians cowered in total darkness (see Exod. 10:21-23); He also leads us by His great light. When God lead His children out of Egypt's darkness He went before them as the pillar of cloud by day, and the pillar of fire by night (see Exod. 13:21). God's light was never removed from their presence. This is why we can depend upon the light of His dreams by night, and His enlightenment by day.

Many stumble because there are areas of darkness in their lives they cannot navigate. These dark areas form strongholds that continually resist growth and progress. When the light of God comes into a dream, the dreamer is often able to clearly receive the truth about a situation for the first time, and the truth breaks the power of the lie that has held that person captive (see 1 John 1:5-7).

When we are held in the captivity of darkness, we lose our hope. The Lord circumcises our ears to hear His voice in the night season through our dreams and visions. His prophetic word enters into our bones and spirit to test and transform us. His Word becomes like water bringing healing to our disjointed, dry bones, and He restores us to abundant life.

Dreams can lead us out of darkness and guide us into God's ever-increasing light. One way to know the path to our future is to embrace the dreams God gives. Dreams will indicate the progress we have made and the work and decisions that are necessary to further our life goals (see Phil. 3:12-16).

Truth will continue to confront the dreamer's soul by causing dreams to reoccur until the truth is embraced. Truth has the power to bring the necessary changes to reality, reforming the character and habits of the soul so that we are able to create the godly life we desire. Dreams only seem impossible when we view them through eyes of fear. When we behold their wisdom with eyes of faith they become a living reality of truth. Forgetting and releasing the painful failures in our past helps us move on to a healthier and happier tomorrow.

When we turn to the Lord, we see Him as He is because the veils of limitation are taken away, and deep calls unto deep (see Ps. 42:7). He is calling for us to be reconnected and united with Him—which is the purpose for which we were created (see 2 Cor. 3:16-18). Veils blind our eyes from seeing the spiritual wisdom and apprehending the revelation knowledge dreams bring. Our desire should be to gaze into the glory and hear the Holy Spirit whispering to our heart. We must seek God's wisdom and revelation to unlock the hidden mysteries that He wants to communicate. The Spirit of the Lord enters our dreams to remove the veils from our hearts and faces so that we will be able to see Him in His transcendent beauty. When we see Him, we will be like Him. He is transforming us from one realm of glory into a higher realm of glory as He reveals Himself to us. We cannot behold Him and continue to live in an unchanged state. As He reveals Himself to us, He is coaching us so that we can understand His mysteries.

There is no time or distance in the Spirit realm. God created time and space for us. The Bible states that one day with the Lord is as a thousand years and a thousand years is as one day. The Holy Spirit can cause us to transcend time and space barriers of the past, present, and future in our dreams by imparting glimpses of the spiritual realm as we sleep. Dreams have the ability to take us out of the natural realms of time. They can move us back into the past, help us to deal with the present, or launch us into the future. The past is history, the future is a mystery, and the present is a gift. That's why they call it a present. Dreams ignite the conscious awareness of our physical, emotional, intellectual, social, and spiritual well-being. Dream symbols come from different areas including our present life, past memories, our subconscious and conscious mind.

Dreams give revelation knowledge that enables us to understand the mysteries sealed in God's heart from the beginning of time. God comes into our dreams to show us who He is in all of His magnificent splendor, love, brilliance, and beauty (see Ps. 65:8-9).

Each time we see God for who He is we are transformed more and more into His image. As we sleep, the Lord comes and helps us transcend our sight, hearing, and our natural minds so that we can see revelation by the Holy Spirit. We are given the knowledge and understanding of mysteries and heavenly beings that we have never imagined. The Spirit of the Lord enables us to step out of the natural realm into the boundless existence of eternity. In the dream realm there are no limitations. We can freely move from the present to the past and even look forward into the future.

WHY DREAMS AND VISIONS?

Paul knew the way of the Spirit. He was translated into the heavenly realms. Because this is true, we can experience this too! In Second Corinthians 12:1-4 Paul spoke of receiving visions and revelation from the Lord. He said that being caught up into the "*third heaven*," and not knowing whether he was in the body or out of the body, was an experience.

He said he experienced "inexpressible things that cannot be put into words, things man is not permitted to tell" (see 2 Cor. 12:4 NIV). He found it difficult to communicate what he saw and experienced in the heavenly realms with his limited vocabulary, and we will too.

John the Revelator was also invited into the realms of the Spirit when he saw a door standing open in Heaven (see Rev. 4:1-2).

John was given an invitation to see the future from a heavenly perspective, but he had to enter the Spirit realm to access the door. Jesus is the door. God is not a respecter of persons. The same invitation that was issued to the apostles Paul and John is being offered to each of us today. So we must learn to navigate the realms of the Spirit in our prayers, dreams, and visions.

God uses dreams to address many issues in our lives to bring us into greater maturity. God's parabolic language in dreams is right in line with the ways He has spoken to people throughout Scripture. We live in a time when Scripture says we will dream dreams, see visions, and prophesy as God pours out His Spirit upon us (see Joel 2:28). The Body of Christ has been given the ability to understand the parables God has hidden in the dreams we dream *and* in the dreams He's given to those who don't know Him yet.

The key to understanding God's dream language is that we must use a biblical basis for interpretation. We rely on the Holy Spirit as our source of revelation, understanding, wisdom, and proper application.

Jesus often taught using parables, which are stories with a deeper spiritual and moral meaning. His disciples asked, *"Why do You speak to them in parables?"* He told them that understanding parables and symbolic imagery is crucial to uncovering the mysteries of the Kingdom (see Matt. 13:10-17). Dreams are basically night parables. The Bible is the first place to look to understand the symbols found in our dreams.

These mysteries are hidden in the realms of the Spirit. Therefore, believers must worship God in Spirit and in truth to enter into this realm of spiritual understanding. It is the Spirit of truth who leads us into all truth (see John 14:17-18).

Dreams are gateways to the supernatural expressions of God. The Holy Spirit comes into our bedchambers to reveal mysteries. There is an urgent call to intimacy with God as never before. The Bible says the marriage bed is undefiled (see Heb. 13:4). You don't let just anyone into the sacred bedchambers—only your covenant lover. Yet, at night the lover of our soul comes to visit us with keys to unlock divine mysteries that are hidden in His heart. He longs to share His secrets with His beloved bride. It is imperative that we learn His love language of dreams. Understanding mysteries of the night will enable us to know His plans and purposes for our life (see Jer. 29:11).

The Holy Spirit comes to reveal the Father and Jesus the Son to us in our dreams (see John 14:23). As we love God wholeheartedly, He will dwell within us and reveal the mysteries of His everlasting Kingdom. Once we understand that God is speaking in our dreams, we will hunger to understand His symbolic language.

Dreams are often a window into divine conversations. Once we learn the symbolic language of dreams, we will begin to walk in an increasing level of understanding of the wisdom being communicated to us. Our God-given dreams hold the answers to the questions we have. Once the correct interpretation is embraced, we have the courage to obey by giving the dream expression.

Deep within the soul of every person is a sense of eternity that can only find fulfillment in knowing God and doing what He created us to do (see Eccles. 3:11).

With God's enlightenment, the dreams we dream become the roadmaps that help direct us to His higher plans. As we call on God, we will begin to comprehend His ways, thoughts, and plans for us revealed in the dreams He gives. Through embracing the changes that our dreams bring, we can walk the new road that God intends for us to walk.

Dreams become the strategic roadmaps that align us with destiny. Dreams contain power that enables us to see what we were created to become. Prophetic dreams reveal God's intended life script, which allows us to walk along His designated path. The Holy Spirit helps direct the dreamer in His waking life to align with His greatest possible destiny.

Dreams allow us to look carefully at our lives from every angle. When our eyes are opened to the ways God sees things, we can see our destiny and the world around us from His perspective. Spiritual understanding is different than natural wisdom. The presence of the Holy Spirit must be resting upon our natural senses of sight, sound, touch, taste, and smell for us to experience the Spirit realm. *Spiritual wisdom* directs us regarding the future. In contrast, *spiritual knowledge* causes us to reflect back on past experiences (both triumphs and failures) through the eyes of God (see Isa. 43:19-21).

A Divine Strategy Waiting to Unfold

This higher road may not always be easy, but it leads to maturity in character and fulfillment of our destiny. We choose this higher spiritual road when we decide to go with God by accepting Jesus and the leading of the Holy Spirit. Throughout our life journey, God continually sensitizes our souls to recognize the ways He wants to speak to us. This path enables us to encounter peace, joy, and fulfillment, and it satisfies our desire to be special, successful, and loved. Along the narrow way, each person discovers a divine strategy waiting to unfold in his or her faith walk. Within every soul is a dream that calls each of us to reflect the image and nature of God. It is like a flower yet unfolding. Our life dreams are calling us to emerge from the cocoon, spread our wings, and catch the breath of God's Spirit, the Holy Spirit, so that we can each soar to the highest heights to become the best we were created to be. God knows the path and the course corrections we need to take when our spirit is overwhelmed (see Ps. 142:3a). Soul dreams call us to change by causing us to objectively look at our mind, will, and emotions as they relate to God, our relationships, health, well-being, and prosperity (see John 17:17).

Dreams reveal the truth of where we are, where we are going, and what obstacles we need to remove to get there. Biblical interpretation enables us to unpack the dream and apply its wisdom to our lives. Dreams can help deliver us from destructive life patterns. Instead of going around the mountain one more time, a new track is laid that takes us into a higher reality. God is establishing His Kingdom in our lives, and He is doing it through dreams and visions. The song between the heart of God and the human spirit and soul has many methods of expression: the Bible; a still small voice; an audible voice; visions; circumstantial confirmations; signs and wonders; and the list continues. God speaks to us through dreams to help us become what we are called to be—productive, responsible, successful, prosperous, loved, and fulfilled. God speaks to the human soul through dreams that influence and challenge our very core. As we accept challenges, we are able to grow and mature in many aspects of life. The life we live here on earth is our training ground for eternity. Every day we are faced with decisions and tests we must overcome with the skills and wisdom we have been given. If any of us lack wisdom, we should ask God who will give us His wisdom without measure.

As our understanding is enlightened with God's wisdom we will be able to follow the leading our dreams provide. Life would be so much smaller if we were not able to dream. So dream freely and see God bring to pass increase, largeness, sufficiency, and a grand future.

About Dr. Barbie L. Breathitt

Dr. Barbie L. Breathitt is an author, television guest, ordained minister, dedicated educator, and respected teacher of the supernatural manifestations of God. Barbie's dynamic teaching skills, intelligence, and quick wit keep her a favorite with audiences everywhere. Through prayer, intense study, and years of research, Barbie has become a recognized leader in dream interpretation and has equipped people in more than 40 nations around the globe. Her prophetic gifting and deep spiritual insights have helped people understand the supernatural ways God speaks.

Books by Barbie L. Breathitt

Dream Encounters

Gateway to the Seer Realm

Dreams and Visions of Destiny

Notes

Printed in Great Britain
by Amazon

41766185R00058